My First Book of Common Wisconsin Birds

by Jean Krieg

Hello!

Thank you for choosing this children's picture book. It is my Wisconsin Master Naturalist Capstone project. For each bird species, I attempted to obtain images of the male, female, nest in a typical habitat, and eggs. If that was not possible, other relevant images were used. In addition, when the male and female of a species are similar in appearance, the top left image is representative.

Jean Krieg

Dedicated to Kayla

Acknowledgements:

Thank you to Wisconsin Master Naturalist instructors Paul Noeldner and Anke Keuser for their knowledge, experience, and inspiration.

Thank you to Anke Keuser for reviewing the images for accuracy.

The bird species represented in this book are the 30 most common Wisconsin birds for years 2012-2016 determined with eBird data.

eBird Basic Dataset. Version: EBD_relMay-2017. Cornell Lab of Ornithology, Ithaca, New York. May 2017.

Image credits are listed at the end of the book.

Copyright © 2017 by Jean Krieg. All rights reserved.
Printed by CreateSpace, an Amazon.com Company
Available from Amazon.com, CreateSpace.com, and other retail outlets
ISBN-13: 978-1976394683
ISBN-10: 1976394686

Black-capped Chickadee

American Crow

American Robin

American Goldfinch

Northern Cardinal

Blue Jay

Mourning Dove

Red-winged Blackbird

Canada Goose

Downy Woodpecker

Mallard

White-breasted Nuthatch

Song Sparrow

Red-bellied Woodpecker

House Sparrow

European Starling

Common Grackle

Dark-eyed Junco

House Finch

Hairy Woodpecker

Sandhill Crane

Ring-billed Gull

Northern Flicker

Gray Catbird

Chipping Sparrow

Tree Swallow

Brown-headed Cowbird

House Wren

Barn Swallow

Red-tailed Hawk

About the Author:

Jean Krieg, a native of Wisconsin, is continually in awe of nature. Read her blog at https://mostlynaturestuff.wordpress.com/.

Wisconsin Master Naturalist: https://www.wimasternaturalist.org/

Resources to learn more about Wisconsin birds:

1. Tekiela, Stan. *Birds of Wisconsin Field Guide*. Cambridge: Adventure Publications, 1999.
2. Porter, Adele. *Wild About Wisconsin Birds: A Youth's Guide to the Birds of Wisconsin*. Cambridge: Adventure Publications, Inc., 2009.

All images were obtained from Shutterstock.com. Credits starting with the top left image and moving in a clockwise direction are as follows:

Black-capped Chickadee: Michael G. Mill, Peter K. Ziminski, Mircea Costina, Feng Yu
American Crow: BGSmith, dreamnikon, Elliotte Rusty Harold, Svetlana Foote
American Robin: Tim Zurowski, Steve Byland, StevenRussellSmithPhotos, Anthony Ricci
American Goldfinch: Tony Campbell, vagabond54, StevenRussellSmithPhotos, Tony Campbell
Northern Cardinal: Merlin Halteman, NSC Photography, Tara Melinda, Ivan Kuzmin
Blue Jay: Bruce MacQueen, Cytis77, Josef Pittner, Juris Kraulis
Mourning Dove: Terry Putman, Coy St. Clair, Ray Hennessy, Bull's-Eye Arts
Red-winged Blackbird: BGSmith, Claudette Cormier, lorenza62, David Byron Keener
Canada Goose: Theresa L. Tanner, NFKenyon, rck_953, kart31
Downy Woodpecker: Andrea J Smith, Jim Nelson, Paul Roedding, Mircea Costina
Mallard: MattParker, Kate Besler, Krymka, Vishnevskiy Vasily
White-breasted Nuthatch: LorraineHudgins, Paul Reeves Photography, Mircea Costina, vagabond54
Song Sparrow: Paul Reeves Photography, Arto Hakola, Andrew Black, Brian E Kushner
Red-bellied Woodpecker: Jim Nelson, Kat Grant Photographer, ClexBennett, Aria_RJWarren
House Sparrow: FotoRequest, Marut Sayannikroth, Roel Slootweg, Michael Schroeder
European Starling: Sharon Day, Mircea Costina, FotoRequest, Voodison328
Common Grackle: Rabbitti, John E Heintz Jr, Noella Kim, John E Heintz Jr
Dark-eyed Junco: Brian E Kushner, Randy R, Lisa Charbonneau, Vibe Images
House Finch: Steve Byland, Paul Reeves Photography, blewulis, Dreamframer
Hairy Woodpecker: FotoRequest, FotoRequest, Donna Allard, Karel Bock
Sandhill Crane: Brian Lasenby, Laurel A Egan, Nagel Photography, Bruce Ellis
Ring-billed Gull: Jim Nelson, Kathryn Carlson, Jim Nelson, D and D Photo Sudbury
Northern Flicker: Ron Rowan Photography, teekaygee, Dan Logan, Mircea Costina
Gray Catbird: Jill Nightingale, Paul Tessier, Brian Lasenby, Beth Van Trees
Chipping Sparrow: Tim Zurowski, Beth Van Trees, Jeramey Lende, FotoRequest
Tree Swallow: Tom Frisby, Steve Byland, Steve Byland, Peter K. Ziminski
Brown-headed Cowbird: NFKenyon, vagabond54, Anatoliy Lukich, Josef Stemeseder
House Wren: Gerald Marella, Katy Foster, John E Heintz Jr, Brian Lasenby
Barn Swallow: HTurner, WildWalker1, Mirko Graul, dilynn
Red-tailed Hawk: Paul Roedding, rck_953, Josef Stemeseder, Paul Reeves Photography

Front cover - Northern Cardinals: Bonnie Taylor Barry
Back cover - American Robin: Hamiza Bakirci